THE SECRET TO FINDING YOUR DREAM PARTNER WITH THE LAW OF ATTRACTION

MANIFEST YOUR TRUE SOULMATE THROUGH THE POWER OF THE UNIVERSE

LANNETTE SEEKER

CONTENTS

INTRODUCTION

What if you could harness the power of the universe and attract the partner of your dreams? If you could take small actions in your daily life that would allow your soulmate to come to you? The Law of Attraction at its most fundamental says that what you think about is what you will attract from the world. If you reflect on the traits and characteristics of your dream partner, together with a little bit of simple work on your part, you can finally meet your soulmate.

If you've picked up this book, then you don't currently have your dream partner in your life. Maybe you have a partner, but they're not fulfilling you in some way. Or you may not have a partner at all, dream or otherwise. You'd rather have your soulmate than someone you just keep company with. Why bother to have a lover in your life if they're not really the one for you?

Do you know who your ideal partner is? Maybe you have a person picked out specifically, but they don't know you exist, or they think of you only as a friend or colleague. Maybe you're not even sure what your dream partner would be like at all! Either way, with the help of this book you'll unlock the secrets of who you're looking for and how to attract them to you.

The tools you'll learn how to use will guide you step-by-step through understanding how the Law of Attraction works. Whether or not you know who you want to bring into your romantic life, you'll discover how to determine what you're looking for. You'll be able to visualize it in enough detail that the universe knows exactly who to send your way. None of these guidelines or tools require you to have any sort of degree, or training, or title, or position. All you need is the willingness to take the necessary actions in order to achieve your dream.

Let's imagine, right now, what your life would be like if you did have your soulmate by your side. You have someone who understands what you need, whether you're at home or out with friends at a party. Someone to share your life with, who's there in the good times and bad. Maybe your dream partner will be a parent to your children. What would it be like to have a co-parent who's completely in harmony with you? You might buy a house together, or travel. How great would it be to retire with your dream partner, spending time in your old age with someone you love so much?

The good news is that this isn't impossible! This isn't some pie-in-the-sky, wild dream that only a select few can achieve. It's true that not everyone is connected with their dream partners. Some have settled for someone that was good enough. Others never thought about what they really wanted, and didn't take the actions necessary to bring it into their lives. But with the help of this book, you can manifest the person who's right for you.

This book teaches you what you need to know to attract your soulmate, whether you're already familiar with the Law of Attraction or not. Even if you know about it, you may not recognize why it's so powerful when it comes to love and romance.

I do have to tell you that there is action needed on your part! I'm providing the required actions and steps that guide you through the process. Although I've done my best to write this book in a way that's easy and fun to read, you won't get the results you've been dreaming about if you only read the book. You have to do the suggested exercises and perform the steps if you want to be successful.

In this book you'll learn about the Law of Attraction (LoA) and how it works. Then you'll discover your dream partner and visualize in enough detail to help attract them to you. After that I introduce the topic of vibration, and how to increase it. This might sound a little crazy at first, but you'll find out what it is. And, why it's so important in your search for a soulmate. Many people encounter hurdles along the way, which may be put up by themselves or by other people. You'll learn about the common ones and more importantly, how you can overcome them. Finally, I teach you how to put everything together to attract the love partner you've always wanted.

Right now you may be wondering why you should read this book, instead of another one. Why am I the right person to guide you through the Law of Attraction and how to use it for your love life? Why should you listen to what I have to say?

Not only am I an expert in the LoA itself, I'm also a relationship and matchmaking guru. I've helped hundreds of people, just like you, who were stuck in a rut. They wanted to find the right person for them, but they got stuck with Mr. or Ms. Right-For-Now. Or they'd opted out of the game entirely, choosing instead to live without a partner because they couldn't find the right one.

I've watched all of these people blossom once they found

Mr. or Ms. Right. Suddenly, with their ideal love match by their side, they've even been able to achieve career goals they never thought they could reach. They've created loving families that light up their lives. They have joy, which is even more important than worldly success.

If you don't have this joy in your life right now, then you've come to the right place. Once you've read the book and taken the actions, you too can find the partner who makes your romantic dreams come true. You too can have the loving family you've always desired.

Why wait? The longer you delay reading this book, the harder it's going to be to attract the right person. They're out there right now waiting for you. They also want the joy of a soulmate and the life they've always dreamed of. So not only are you hurting yourself by waiting to learn how to use the Law of Attraction, you're hurting them too!

Manifesting your ideal partner is exciting, and improves your life. What do you have to lose? Get started right now and attract your soulmate!

Before we get into the discussion of how you can adopt the power of the universe to find your dream partner, we need to talk about what the Law of Attraction (LoA) is and what it is not. The basic concept behind it has been known by humans for centuries, but its modern form became clearer in the early 20th century.

The Law of Attraction is helpful for many different people who want to manifest a variety of things, such as career success. It's also very powerful when it comes to love. Once you've found your soulmate using the techniques in this book, you can come back to this process and repeat it for other areas of your life where you want to have more success.

The early years of the Law of Attraction

The roots of the law are seen even in pre-Christian times. Buddha says, "All that we are is a result of what we have thought." It's believed that humanity has always had some sense of this teaching, though it wasn't until the 1900s and a famous spiritual medium named Helena Blavatsky that the Law of Attraction came to be named (Hurst, 2019).

In the early 20th century, there were several books written about the law and how to use it to get rich. One of them remains one of the most popular books ever written, <u>Think and Grow Rich</u>, by Napoleon Hill (VOA, 2012). The LoA continues to capture the public imagination in a number of fields.

What's the basis of the LoA?

Whatever you focus on is what you bring into your life. What you give your attention and energy to is what will come back to you. From this fundamental principle, you can see that if you are constantly thinking about negative things, that you'll receive negativity in your life. Sometimes it's hard to break the habits of negative thinking! But if you want to have the things you truly desire, you need to make a shift to positivity.

Have you ever heard of the phrase "like attracts like"? That's the LoA in a nutshell. If you're sending out high energy, positive, abundant, appreciative vibes, then that's what the universe responds to. If you're feeling ungrateful, resentful, joyless, or anxious… well, you get the picture. It's not the universe's job to decide what kind of energy is best for you and to send it to you. Rather, it responds to the vibrations that you provide it.

What are you thinking and feeling, right now? You're asking the universe for more of that, whatever it is. Even if you didn't realize you were asking it for anything. The request doesn't have to be in the form of an actual question. It can just be the energy that's emanating from you.

USING THE LAW OF ATTRACTION

Now that you know you're making requests without perhaps even meaning to, you can choose what you want to ask for. Sometimes this means making a mindset shift. If you tend to be suspicious and doubt that good things will come your way - guess what, you're right! But if you decide that you're going to open up your mind and heart to the possibilities of positive thinking, you're on your way to getting your heart's desire.

When it comes to your own mindset, there's actually some neuroscience that can help you be more positive. You may have heard about *neuroplasticity*, which just means that our neurons (brain cells) adapt to their environment. While we sleep or are otherwise unconscious, the brain prunes back pathways between neurons if they're not being used very much. It can also strengthen the pathways that are being used a lot. This is why people tell you to "sleep on it" when you have a big decision to make or test to take.

Do you habitually think in terms of the negative? That you can't have what you want, or you'll never find the right person, or you'll never find the right job that makes you money, or that the world is unfair to you? Those are the pathways that your brain strengthens while you sleep. You use them often, which makes them stronger, which means you default to those thoughts. Which makes them stronger, and on and on.

The good news is that you're not doomed to negative thinking forever! Remember, brain cells adapt. If you catch yourself thinking something negative and replace it with something positive, you're disrupting that pathway. As you get better and better about seeing the good in your situation, the less those negative pathways get used. Your brain will start pruning them back more. We'll discuss affirmations and positive psychology later in the book, but for now, just recognize that you may need to shift your mindset to bring your dream partner into your life. See if you can catch yourself thinking these negative thoughts as you go about your day. Can you think of anything positive to replace them?

Maintaining abundant and affirmative energy is part of the three-step procedure for manifesting what you want (Canfield, 2019).

1. Ask for what you want, not what you don't

Given that the LoA works on what you think about and spend your energy on, don't waste your time thinking about things you don't want! In the next chapter you'll go through an exercise of finding out what is desirable in an ideal lover and what isn't. But don't dwell on the "don't want" aspects.

Think positive. What do you want? Suppose you want a partner who likes children. Don't ask for someone who merely doesn't avoid them, or who doesn't dislike them. Formulate your request in positive terms. Think of someone who loves children, who treats them well, who treats their nieces and nephews well, who enjoys seeing pictures of happy kids.

2. Believe you can receive, then take action

If you don't truly believe that you can have what you want, you're right. Sometimes this can be the hardest part of the LoA. You figure out who your ideal partner is, and you think you've set yourself up for success. But you don't actually believe that your desire will be brought into your life.

Maybe there's a part of you that thinks you're not good enough, or maybe you still suspect that the world is against you. These are known as "limiting beliefs", and they will prevent you from achieving whatever it is you've asked for.

To be truly prepared to take action, you must know in your heart that yes, you're good enough. And no, the world is not out to get you. You act on the steps to create the result that you want, knowing that it's within your reach.

3. Match what you want through vibration

In other words, develop that positive reaction. Practice feeling the emotions that you'll feel once you get what you want: love, happiness, joy. Your thoughts create your feelings, so thinking good thoughts will help you with the emotions too.

Is this easy? For many people, not at all. But it is possible. The more you practice, the better you'll be. And that much closer to your dreams.

ABUNDANCE

This concept is key to the Law of Attraction. It means that there is enough of what you need in the universe. Enough love, enough joy, enough money for everyone. Therefore, there is certainly enough of whatever it is that you're trying to attract into your life.

You need to know that this is true in order to have that partner you've been dreaming of. The opposite of abundance is scarcity or lack of resources. When people have a scarcity mindset, they're not able to open their minds and eyes to the opportunities that are in front of them. They're worried that there isn't enough to go around, and they're often stressed and fearful.

Scarcity holds people back from achieving their full

potential. They're less willing to take risks, which are necessary to get out of your comfort zone and live fully. People who don't believe in abundance are worried about losing money or time. They're constantly struggling and competing to be the best and get the most they can. They play the victim and are always blaming others for their failures, and get stuck in negativity.

When you believe in abundance, you operate out of self-confidence and security. Knowing there's plenty to go around means you don't feel the need to compete with anyone to be the best version of yourself that you can be. Except maybe yourself. You see all the possibilities that exist for you, and take advantage of opportunities when they appear. Most importantly for bringing your ideal mate into your life, you think positively.

MANIFESTATION

You've probably heard people talking about manifesting what they want. But what does it mean exactly? The term comes up a lot when discussing the LoA, so it's important to know what it is and why it's so powerful.

Manifesting something means that it's brought into physical or actual reality through feelings, beliefs and thoughts. In this book I'll show you how to manifest your dream partner, but you also might want to manifest a dream job career too, for example.

As mentioned above, negativity attracts negativity. In order to manifest your ideal, you'll need to be thinking constructively. Manifestation also requires action. If your desire was a dream job, then you'd need to apply for jobs, go on interviews, network, etc. In this book we're focusing on your ideal partner. Which means making yourself available for dating, going to places where you might find someone with the qualities you want, and so forth.

Suppose you're looking for a mate who enjoys skiing as much as you do. Where would you go? To the slopes, naturally! Ski resort towns, maybe even skiing conferences or trade shows. You'd let your friends who are skiers know that you're looking for a partner who skis. You might even buy another ski suit, or some other ski equipment, to symbolize the partner you'll be attracting.

ATTRACTING YOUR SOULMATE

Although the Law of Attraction is beneficial in many different situations, it's particularly helpful when it comes to romance. Love is one of those emotions that never runs out. In fact, the more love you give, the more you have to give and the more you receive. If you want an abundance of love in your life, then you must give love.

That doesn't mean you have to physically love every person who crosses your path! But you can be compassionate and kind and generous to other human beings.

By now, depending on how long you've been waiting for your dream partner, you may be feeling unloved or unloveable. You may be lonely. It's pretty common for people who haven't yet discovered their soulmate to feel this way, so don't despair. You need to know that you are loveable and that you are enough. Many people need to do some work in this area in order to be ready to receive their gift from the universe, and we'll talk about those methods later.

As humans we create our own experiences and our own selves. We need to love ourselves before we make the transformation into loving others, so that's the first step. You'll also need to put yourself out there. The universe can't teleport your dream partner right to your doorstep, unfortunately! Make yourself available, and apply yourself to personal growth too. Find a pool of people to swim in who are also trying to stay in a positive mindset, working to improve themselves, and open to what the universe has to provide. You can do this in person at parties, networking or other social gatherings, but also make sure you're open on social media too on your chosen platform(s).

Be aware that this process will take some time. You won't read this book, decide you love yourself, and then have your soulmate knocking the door asking to marry you the next day! Desperation is not only a turn-off to potential lovers, it's a sign that you doubt that you'll achieve your result. Allow the process to work. You'll be thinking good thoughts and feeling good as you work on your own personal development. Which will make you even more attractive to your dream partner once they've entered your circle.

Chapter Summary

When using the Law of Attraction to manifest your dream partner, you need to stay positive and avoid negativity as much as you can.

- The LoA has been around for centuries, though only in the past two have people really come to understand its power.
- It is based on the idea that you will receive into your life what you put out into the universe.
- You can use the Law of Attraction in many different areas of life, but you have to be ready first.
- Manifesting your dreams is bringing them into

physical reality from your thoughts, and it also requires you to take some action to make it work.
- The LoA works for manifesting your dream partner, as well as for other dreams you may have.

IN THE NEXT CHAPTER YOU WILL LEARN ABOUT YOUR own personal dream partner.

CHAPTER TWO: WHO IS YOUR DREAM PARTNER?

Now that you understand the Law of Attraction (LoA) and how it works, you're ready to start thinking about your ideal lover and bring them into your life. You may not know who your soulmate is right this second, and that's OK. By the end of this chapter you'll have enough detail to visualize them. And you'll know which actions to take to begin the process of manifesting them.

What you bring to the relationship

Ever heard the phrase, "Know thyself"? You have to start here to properly manifest your dreams. What are your own qualities? It helps to write them down.

If you like, you can use a special notebook for using the LoA to find your soulmate. When you write things down instead of typing them, you'll actually retain the information better (Holly, 2020). Plus, actually writing things down gives you something to look at and come back to when you need it.

Go ahead and write down everything you bring to the

relationship you'll have with your soulmate. No matter how small and silly, make sure you wrote it down. Great at making pancakes? Best at putting together outfits for work? The funny faces you make that your dog likes? Write them down, in addition to your other qualities: loyal, funny, smart, reliable, unpredictable, spontaneous, adventurous, having a love of learning, etc.

If you come up with negative qualities or issues, that's OK. Don't mix them up with the great things that you bring, though. Keep them separate and consider whether those are things you need to work on for the future. Make sure that you have more affirmative qualities on your list. Dig deep if you need to! If you run dry, you can always ask supportive friends and family for the characteristics they like about you, and write those down too.

TRY A T-CHART

Now it's time to discover what qualities you want in your soulmate! You may know some of them already. In your special notebook or on a blank sheet of paper, draw a line down the middle of the paper vertically so you have a T shape. Label the left column "Don't Want" and the right column, "Do Want".

If you already have some ideas about what you do and don't want, write them down in the appropriate columns. For now it's OK if your "Don't Want" list is longer, though ultimately you need more details on the other side.

Many people find it easier to write down what they don't want, at first. For everything that you don't want in a dream mate, make sure you write down what the positive equivalent is on the right side. Suppose you don't want someone who smokes. You'd write that in the left column, and in the right you could transform that idea into someone who doesn't smoke, or even better, someone who lives a healthy lifestyle. If you *don't* want a couch potato, you *do* want someone who maintains an active lifestyle.

If you come up with positive qualities, there's no need to make a corresponding negative one. You know by now that you're going to focus on the constructive traits. Having a hard time figuring out what you do and don't want, or feel like you have a short list? Look back on your relationships in the past.

If you haven't had many romantic ones, that's OK. Consider your friendships too. What did you like about those people? Would you want those traits in your soulmate? If there was something you didn't like, how can you turn it into an affirmative quality that goes on the right side of your list?

Once you believe you've written down everything you can think of for an ideal mate, look at the right side of the T. Think about a person who has all of these qualities. Ask yourself if this type of person is really what you want, in your heart of hearts. Can you imagine spending the rest of your life with this person? Does it feel right?

If the answer to these questions are all "yes", you're good to go. If the answer to one or more is "no", then you'll need to do a little more work. Are you missing something? Or is one (or more) of the traits you've written down not something that you want, but that you think others want for you?

Maybe your parents want you to settle down with someone who has a steady job. But really you want someone with a sense of adventure who can just pack up and go traveling with you. To attract your dream partner, you don't want to manifest your parents' idea of your soulmate. Or the type of person your friends think you should go after. It won't happen. You have to believe that this person, with these qualities, is the person that you could spend the rest of your life with. If you've listed things that don't speak to you, you're not attracting your dream partner.

You don't have to tell anyone what you want, either. This isn't a committee exercise. It's for you, and you alone. Whatever your secret desires are, write them down. Once you can answer "yes" to all the questions, you're ready to finish your T chart.

Cross off every single one of the "Don't Want" items on your list. Sometimes it's a lot of fun to use a very fat dark marker so you can't even see what was written there. It's very therapeutic for some people! Those are all the qualities that you're going to ignore. You will be focusing on the positive qualities: the things that you actively do want to bring forth into your life.

VISUALIZATION

This is an extremely powerful technique, and many people don't understand just how impressive it actually is. Many people use it, including elite athletes. Olympians frequently incorporate visualization into their training strategies. It turns out that imagining something in your mind's eye, with lots of detail, activates the brain in the same way that performing the action in reality does.

There's another robust neuroscientific reason that visualization is so important. We humans are bombarded with images and sights and sounds and smells all day every day, and our brains filter out a lot of it. Just so we don't go crazy from all the sensory input. Visualizing something tells the brain to pay attention to it, so it won't be automatically filtered out with all the other things (Palmer, n.d.)

Have you noticed that after you've bought a car, or are looking to buy a specific car, that all of a sudden you see them all over the road? It's the same concept. From your search for a specific car, your brain realized it needed to pay attention to it, and the filtration mechanism stopped blocking it out.

Visualization engages this same concept. The brain has been told to pay attention to a specific sort of person. It will stop filtering out people who have those traits. That's why it's so important when you're seeking your soulmate. If one of the qualities you desire is for humor, you'll suddenly notice how funny people are when you meet them, because your brain is paying attention to it.

When performing your visualization, it's best to be alone somewhere quiet. You need to pour all your energy into it, so you'll need to be free of distractions. You don't have to spend a lot of time on it, maybe just a minute or two. But make that minute count! Ensure that your mind picture is as real as it can possibly be as to what the outcome feels, smells, sounds, and tastes like. The more vivid the picture, the better it is.

Don't worry about how you're going to get there. The specific steps to take in order to manifest your dream partner aren't important in the visualization. Also, who will bring the person to you is not anything to consider while you're imagining your soulmate. The key here is to see the outcome in your mind's eye, as clearly as you possibly can. Almost like it's already yours.

In order for your visualization to be most effective, there are three practices that will make the most of it.

1. Rich in detail

The more specific you can be about your soulmate, the better. You may have particular physical characteristics that you need in a partner, so "see" those in your mind's eye. Bear in mind, however, that they tend not to be as important as internal or mental characteristics such as kindness or bravery.

Think about what the nonphysical characteristics really mean to you. What does "brave" mean? Can you envision a situation where your partner is brave? People view bravery differently, so make sure that you yourself know exactly how your partner would be brave with you. Make these scenarios as rich as possible too. What do they smell and sound like?

2. Feel the emotions

This is a specific detail that you need to bring to your visualizations. How will you feel when this person is by your side? Happy, content, excited, loving, romantic…? This isn't a math problem you're trying to solve. Let your imagination run wild when it comes to emotions. Feelings are very powerful both in life and in your mind's picture.

3. Often

It helps to have this richly imagined detail front and center, reminding your brain what it needs to pay attention to and reminding you why you're doing this work. Once a day is the bare minimum for doing a visualization of your soulmate, but two or three times daily is even better.

Vision board

One way to make visualization easier is to create a vision board that gives tangible evidence of your image. Then you have the picture of your ideal partner in front of you at all times. The more familiar you are with something, the more confident you'll be that you will achieve it.

If you've never made a vision board before, this may not

seem like an important thing to do. But you probably have made visual representations of something that you wanted. For example, have you ever cut out a picture in a magazine of clothing you wanted to buy? Or room decor that you wanted for your own home? Have you ever been out shopping and taken a photo (maybe even a selfie) of something desirable? Most people have.

A vision board is a place to put these reminders of what you want all in one place where you can't miss it. It's a collection of items that you curate to help you manifest your dream. In this case, your dream partner. It helps you get in tune with your ideal mate, and encourages you to think positively.

Everything on your board should be something that you want, so that you're focusing on your desires with nothing negative in the picture. By immersing yourself in the idea of your ideal future, you'll automatically increase your vibrational energy (more about this in the next chapter). It helps you avoid or decrease the time you spend in limiting beliefs. Seeing the images of your soulmate and your life with them reinforces the idea that this is absolutely possible. And for you specifically.

Putting together a vision board can be very simple. It doesn't have to take much work to create such a powerful tool for attracting your soulmate. There are tutorials and online articles available, but it doesn't require specialized skill. You don't need to have any artistic talent, either. All you need is the picture you have of your ideal partner.

- *Background*

Before computers, people put their vision boards together physically, using something like a cork board or magnetic board. You could use a large sheet of paper too. Or an entire wall if you like. Just as with visualization, the more detail the better.

You can now do your board on a computer as well, which some people prefer. Getting away from your computer to put things together with your own hands is more satisfying for many, but this is your vision board. Choose the method that works best for you.

- *Pictures*

Any kind of image will work. You might want to include inspirational quotes, talking about love or the kind of relationship you dream of having. The items don't have to be photos either. Some people use special stones or feathers or cardboard, if you're making a physical as opposed to digital vision board. You can cut out pictures from magazines and newspapers, or print out images you find online.

Plus, you don't have to use images that others have made. You can draw, write, take your own photos. Whatever is positive and supports your goal of finding your dream partner will work. Be as creative as you like. Or not! You can start off with less and add more as you go or find inspiration as you proceed along your journey.

- *Set up for success*

After you've collected your images, at least to start with, and selected your background, make sure that you're creating your vision board in a serene environment that makes you feel confident. Give yourself enough time so that you don't feel rushed.

It's helpful to treat this as a ritual in your Law of Attraction practice. Maybe you want to meditate briefly at the beginning, or light a candle. Calm music or other soothing sounds are good too. You want to be able to focus your intent on what you're doing.

Gather your images, words, background, glue, and anything else you might want to feature on your board: washi tape, stickers, glitter, etc.

- *Action*

Now you're ready to create! A vision board doesn't have to be perfectly laid out and neat and tidy. Unless that's part of the dream partner that you're manifesting. No need for a narrative as to how you set up your pictures, unless you naturally find one as you look through the images that you've chosen.

Your vision board is not a place to overthink. You're tapping into different wisdom instead of your logical brain. This is a time to trust your intuition and to place images in ways that feel good or "right". Even if you can't say or don't know why it's good and right.

- *Repeat*

No, you don't have to keep creating vision boards. Unless it's something that you really enjoy doing! What you need to repeat is the habit of studying your vision board for just a few minutes a day.

Experiment with the best times to look at your board. Some people like to look at it before they go to bed at night. They prime their unconscious mind to work on it while they sleep. Others like to study theirs first thing in the morning so they can set the intention to manifest their soulmate each day. Or you may find another time of day that works better for you.

It's also helpful to update it regularly. You might find new images that catch your attention as you go about your day. Make sure you put them on your board. Or new words that you want to add that will help you focus.

Chapter Summary

Once you have decided on the attributes of your dream partner, use visualization tools to help you manifest The One.

- First you need to know what you will bring to your dream partner relationship.
- Write down all the things that you want and don't want in your soulmate, and then cross off all the negative attributes.
- Visualize the positive attributes of your ideal mate several times a day.
- Use a vision board to make your dreams concrete, and study it once a day.

In the next chapter you will discover the secrets of vibration.

CHAPTER THREE: RAISE YOUR VIBRATION

Everything in the universe vibrates. Yes, even stones and desks and the vision board you made in the last chapter. All matter is made of energy, because deep within, millions of subatomic particles are moving. The vibrational energy is known as resonance, and each person has their own frequency.

You already know that like attracts like, and that the universe will give you what you put into it. When you're in your natural state, with your natural frequency, you'll be able to manifest what you want. It's when you're out of resonance that you may manifest things you don't want.

WHY ARE PEOPLE OUT OF THEIR NATURAL FREQUENCY?

You've seen how joyful children are when they're young. They haven't been told that there are things they can't do, and their imaginations are limitless. But as people grow older, they may be told by parents and/or teachers that they can't do certain things, and shouldn't even attempt them.

The authority figures may mean well (they don't always). The end result, however, is that many people are programmed to think about ideas such as shame, scarcity, inadequacy, worry and fear instead of more affirming emotions. If this is you, don't worry! There are ways that you can rise above your programming. You'll learn how to raise your vibration back to where it should be.

POSITIVE AFFIRMATIONS

One way to raise your vibration is to regularly think and say positive affirmations to yourself. These are short, positive statements that help you focus on the positive and discard the negative.

Human beings think hundreds, if not thousands, of thoughts every day. The brain doesn't know whether these thoughts are true or helpful. It just creates them. If you have a lot of negative thoughts, you're building up negative neural pathways that make unconstructive thinking a habit. Positive affirmations are a way to counter these old pathways and start building new ones that will help you attract your dream partner.

Just as with visualization, you need to repeat affirmations at least once a day in order for them to take hold. They're called positive affirmations, not negative affirmations, for a reason. Make sure the affirmations you use don't have any negative or limiting belief language in them. Make a list of several that you can use on a regular basis. They'll help you actively counter the negative tapes that run in your head.

State affirmations in the past tense, as if they've already happened. Or in the present, meaning that they're happening right now. Don't use the future tense, as in "I will". Don't worry about how you're going to make the affirmations come true, because that's not the point of the affirmation. Just use statements that describe your ideal life with your ideal mate.

You might choose to say something like:

- "I spread love to all around me and it returns to me with abundance."
- "I welcome love with open arms."
- "Love is attracted to me and I am attracted to love."
- "I am loveable just as I am."
- "I deserve love."
- "My relationships are safe and fulfilling."
- "Love is my birthright."
- "I am grateful for the love in my life."
- "I love myself unconditionally."

These are just a few examples. You can make your own list with anything that makes you feel more confident and more ready to receive your dream partner.

Some people find affirmations like this difficult, and that's OK too. If you don't think they're believable or realistic, you just need to make a little tweak to your statements.

"I'm *beginning* to believe that love is attracted to me and I am attracted to love." "I'm *becoming* loveable just as I am." "I am *allowing* myself to deserve love." Affirmations like these often feel more realistic to people who are new to the concept. Even so, they still allow you to focus on the positive in the current moment.

POSITIVE THINKING EXERCISES

Just as affirmations help you to focus on your positive intent, you can also learn to think in a way that will help you raise your vibrational energy. The more optimistic you are, the higher your vibration. You can practice these exercises regularly. Pick some to do when you start feeling a little self-doubt or negativity creeping in as well. These should be done in addition to the positive affirmations as described above.

- *Deep breathing*

There's a feedback loop between your body and mind. Your brain may get freaked out about something, and you can use your body to calm it down. The mind-body connection is a two-way street. When you start feeling anxious or stressed, remember that you can make changes to your body that will soothe your mind as well.

Breathing is one of the ways that you can use your body to calm down your "monkey brain". Best of all, it can be done anywhere: in the car, at the grocery store, at home. It's nice to do it when you're by yourself so you can close your eyes, because that helps to soothe the brain faster.

There are many deep breathing exercises, but here are two that are easy to remember. With either one, breathe very deeply from the bottom of your torso. Shallow, fast breathing signals that you're stressed, so you need to do the opposite.

1. Threes

Inhale slowly for a count of three, hold for a count of three, then exhale for a count of three. Do this three times (or more if you need more soothing.)

2. Box Breathing

Inhale for a count of five, hold for a count of five, exhale for a count of five, and then hold for a count of five. Repeat until you feel less stressed.

- *Smile*

Another mind-body trick when your mind is trending negative is to smile. Even if it's kind of a fake smile at first. Smiling tells your mind that you're happy, and the brain responds by releasing "happy" neurotransmitters like serotonin and dopamine. Maybe it feels cheesy, and that's OK. It's one of the few times where fake it 'til you make it actually works.

- *The Mirror Exercise*

Twice a day (morning and night), stand in front of a mirror and tell yourself what you like about yourself. Find something to say each time. You appreciate how strong your thighs and hips are. You have a great sense of humor, or you're reliable, etc. Let yourself know how wonderful you are!

As always, leave out the negativity and the "if only"s. There may be things you'd like to improve, but this time is for praising yourself. And no backhanded compliments either. No "but"s.

- *Let go of the past*

Easy, right? Well, there's nothing you can do about what happened to you in the past, or actions that you took that maybe don't look so great in hindsight. However, every experience is valuable as long as you learn from it. Take what you can from the past to help you propel forward into the future. Leave the rest behind where it belongs.

- *Perform random acts of kindness*

Very few things will make you feel better than helping others. You can help someone who's struggling to carry their groceries (make sure you ask permission first.) Move a turtle off the sidewalk and onto the grass so it won't get run over by people not paying attention. Pay for the coffee of the person behind you. Call up someone you haven't spoken to for a while and let them know you're thinking about them and wishing them well. What else can you come up with?

- *Do something you love*

One way to feel incredible is to do something you absolutely love! Reading, crafting, dancing, listening to music, whatever floats your boat. Try to make it active instead of passive. Create something instead of shopping for a finished product (even if you need to buy materials for it.) Avoid watching TV or movies or content that someone else has produced if you can.

- *Write a gratitude list*

What are you grateful for? They might be small things, like no traffic on the way to work or that you found a great watermelon at the market. Or they could be big things: you're grateful that you and your family are healthy. Make sure you write it down. If you like you can repeat them out loud too.

- *Fill your mind with positive ideas and thoughts*

This is a great way to crowd out the negativity that's too often the mind's default. The human brain can focus on just one idea at a time. So if you're thinking negative thoughts, intentionally start thinking positive ones and the negative ones have to go away.

Any positive thoughts are good. If you have trouble coming up with any, you can repeat some of your affirmations. You can also try just thinking about things you like, or remembering happy memories from the past, or even dreaming about a bright future.

- *Read inspiring material*

You can read books by or about people who inspire you. There may be magazine articles that you find inspiring. Whatever it is, immerse yourself in it. This works really well if the story is about someone who had to overcome hurdles in life and succeeded.

- *Create a personal mantra*

This could be a word or phrase, anything that inspires and motivates you. You can repeat it to yourself while meditating, but also when you're stuck in a tricky situation.

- *Use positive words when thinking and talking*

Try to erase negative words like can't, won't, don't, etc. from your vocabulary. Know what others are negative? Words like should or ought. Strike these from your vocabulary and focus on what you are doing and what you can do.

Try to increase your use of rich detail in words, too. If you step outside and see a beautiful landscape in front of you, describe it using strong words. Not pretty or nice, but wonderful or inspiring. The trees are emerald green, or possibly pine green, or maybe even spring green. Not just "green".

- *Create a high-vibration morning routine*

Have you heard that it's bad for you to roll over and check your phone/email first thing in the morning? Usually the time after you awaken is one of the most productive of the day. By checking your email you're squandering this valuable resource of time (Seagraves, 2018). Plus, now you've given up your day to someone else. You're probably comparing yourself negatively to the images you see and thinking about what you've missed since the previous day.

Does that sound like it raises your vibration? Of course not. The best thing is to have your phone in a different room from where you sleep. Buy a cheap alarm clock if you need an alarm to get up in the morning.

Your vibration is at rest while you sleep, so your morning routine helps you set a high vibration for the rest of the day. Assuming that you do it right! Have a positive routine, which may include any of the following: affirmations, exercise, hydration, nourishment, gratitude.

If you're new to a good morning routine, start with deep breaths and gratitude before you do anything else for the day.

- *Surround yourself with positive people*

Stay away from Negative Nancy and Debbie Downer! The more you associate yourself with people who want to lift you up, and be lifted up themselves, the more optimistic you'll be. If you do have downers in your life, minimize contact with them as best you can.

Manifesting meditations

Meditation is a way to create space for positivity in your mind. It's a relaxation technique that helps you feel good and also calms your mind. Both are important tools for manifesting your dream partner. It's best done in a quiet, serene place where there won't be a lot of startling noise to bother you. If you can't find a quiet place, then find the quietest place you can.

Sit or lie down comfortably and light a candle if you wish. Newbies to meditation should start with short periods of time. If you try to meditate for an hour your first few times out, you're going to end up very frustrated and not feeling calm at all. Start with a few minutes (use a timer.)

In general, meditation is about focus. Many people start with the breath, but others might use a mantra. You don't want to change the breath in any way, but let it happen naturally and notice what all the sensations.

The crucial thing to know about meditation is that your thoughts are going to intrude. They are. It doesn't mean you're doing it wrong. Just that your brain is doing what it does naturally.

However, you don't want to attach yourself or any meaning to these thoughts. Your brain made them up, but they're not relevant to your meditation. Some people put the intruding thoughts on (mental) clouds that come and go in the sky. Others place them on a leaf in their imagination that then meanders down the stream. The thoughts will come, and the thoughts will go. Once the thought has floated away, gently come back to your breath or mantra.

That means you don't get angry with your mind for doing mind things! It happened. Let it go, and now be ready to return to your focus.

There are all types of meditation that you can practice. If you have a hard time with your monkey brain ceaselessly chattering away, you might benefit from guided meditation. There's someone who guides you through what to focus on during the meditation, via apps or videos. It's not just you trying to focus on your breath and feeling like you're failing miserably.

Combine meditation with visualization for a very powerful manifesting meditation. It's sort of a guided one, because you'll be creating a loose script to follow for your meditation.

After you're in your preferred meditation posture, relax. Many people like to clench and then relax their muscle groups, starting with their toes and working their way up to the head. Once you've gone through your whole body, notice if there are still any tense parts. Squeeze and relax them if so.

Now focus on your breathing. Remember, don't change or alter it, just notice it. This will probably take a few minutes until you're completely in tune with it. Before you continue on with the rest of the meditation, you'll need to make sure you have love and positive intent in your heart.

You can repeat something like, "My heart is open. I open my heart. I am good, I do good, and I am loved." Or, "I am worthy. I am cared for and care for others. I love myself, and I love others" (Kaplan, 2017). This helps you relax and be more focused. Do this for several minutes also.

Now, visualize your dream partner. Recall the positive traits that you wrote down in your T-chart. Think about what you added to your vision board. Imagine what your life is like now that you have this person in your life. As always, the more detail the better. Use all your senses. Feel the sunshine on your skin as your soulmate joins you in your preferred activity (or raindrops if that's more your speed!) Hear the happy giggles of your children, if that's part of the manifestation. Stop and smell the roses, literally.

Having a hard time remembering the script, or letting

your thoughts go, or having any other issues with the meditation when you sit down to do it yourself? Try a guided meditation. You'll find meditations for manifesting your ideal partner on most of the apps available and also on YouTube or other streaming services.

This is a powerful technique for manifesting your dreams. Make sure that you incorporate this into your practice. Use a guide if you're uncomfortable doing it yourself. Just make sure you practice this manifesting meditation regularly.

Physical connection

So far much of what we've discussed in raising your vibration is mental or emotional. Using your mind to draw rich pictures of life with your dream partner. Practicing gratitude and affirmations, using thoughts and words to accentuate the positive and remove negative thoughts and images from our minds.

But using your body and your senses to raise your vibration is important too. Some of the ways you can manifest your desire also make you feel good and are good for your body. Anything that brings you true joy will help you get back to your natural frequency and attract your soulmate. Crafts and hobbies that you genuinely love will make you feel more optimistic. If you can find groups of others who enjoy the same craft, even better. That puts you into a pool of people where you may find your ideal partner.

There are other ways that involve movement and the senses that raise your vibration and send the signal to the universe that you're ready.

- *Yoga*

There are many different types of yoga practiced today. Most of them raise your vibrational frequency. Yoga poses, or asanas, help you open your body and release tension. Some people find that after long practice, they can perform physical exercises they never thought they could.

Flexibility increases with yoga. You may have some limitations in your body, but you can still increase your flexibility. Which also helps you increase your frequency. Or you may be very flexible already, and yoga can help you maintain that through time.

Another important way that yoga helps raise your vibration is through the breathwork. Some yoga practices focus almost exclusively on the breath, but most at minimum incorporate an acknowledgement of the breath as you move through the poses.

- *Exercise*

Getting your blood pumping is a great way to increase your vibe. You probably know already that it's good for your body. And it's good for your mind. Exercise helps increase your blood circulation, so your brain also gets the benefits of oxygen-rich blood. Some people even get the "runner's high" where the brain starts releasing happy chemicals like serotonin and dopamine.

Even if your brain doesn't release endorphins, exercise is still a mood boost. You'll feel better about yourself and your body when you move it regularly and strengthen it.

You don't have to do any specific type of exercise to reap the benefits of vibrational frequency. Just get everything moving on a regular basis. Dance party for one!

If you haven't been exercising, start small and go slow. If you're exercising already, great! Try something new to mix it up and keep your vibe high. Try a new type of class or use a different set of weights. There are plenty of workouts available on most streaming platforms and YouTube.

- *Nourish yourself*

A dehydrated person is a low vibration person. It's something that many people don't think about. Except maybe for those of us who live in the desert. If you're getting headachy and sluggish, it might not be hunger. You may just need to drink more water.

If you don't like cold water, get a pretty decanter and leave your water out at room temperature. Put it in the fridge or add ice if you prefer it cold. Don't like the taste of your tap water? Or is it too dangerous to drink (this is only true for a handful of places in the US)? Use a filter. You can also infuse it with fruit or a no-sugar-added flavoring if you need a little more oomph in your H2O.

Make sure you bring some with you when you go out. Avoid buying bottled water for this purpose. It costs money that you don't need to spend. Additionally, plastic bottles are bad for the Earth, which means the universe doesn't like it either! Get a cute refillable container and use it.

The food you eat also has an effect on your vibrational frequency. Anything that causes inflammation in the body is going to lower it. Eating fried foods, those with added sugar, and overly processed foods all send a signal to the universe that you're not ready for your dream partner.

Instead, eat the foods that make you feel good after you've eaten them. That don't make you sluggish or send you on a blood sugar rollercoaster. Nourishing yourself this way raises your vibration and makes you feel good.

You'll also want to eliminate, or at least decrease, alcohol and other toxins in your body. A high vibration person doesn't numb themselves in response to stressful situations.

It's the same thing as telling the universe that it can't take care of you. By now you know what that means. Clear out the booze and any other toxins and raise your vibration.

Just like with inflammatory food, cutting out toxins entirely is best and will raise your frequency much better than simply decreasing it. But if you can't go cold turkey, then reducing the amount of low-vibration chemicals is a good start.

- *Live "as if"*

Think about what your life would be like with your dream partner in it. Arrange your living space to accommodate this person. Do you need additional seating? Instead of a chair to watch TV in, maybe you need a loveseat for the two of you to sit in. If you sleep in a twin bed, your soulmate does not have room! You're going to need a bigger bed.

Make sure your space is beautiful, too. It boosts your own energy and makes space for another beautiful person to be in it. You may want to paint the walls a different color that soothes you and makes you feel at home. Get better lighting if necessary so you can see your true love's face clearly.

Get rid of clutter or things you're not using and don't expect to use when your dream partner arrives. Donate or sell clothing you no longer wear, or never have worn. The more space you have, the better you'll feel. And by opening up your living areas, you're making space for your dream partner.

- *Music*

Playing an instrument, or even singing karaoke, can be a high-vibe activity. If you don't, listening to music is an excellent way to raise your frequency. But you do need to be choosy about the kind of music you listen to, as well as the movies and TV shows that you watch.

Is there a lot of violence in the lyrics, or hatred, or any other low-vibration attributes to what you're listening to? This is common (though not exclusive to) country, gangster rap, and death metal. Curate your playlist so you're listening to upbeat, positive forms of music. Maybe try some like EDM or classical that have no lyrics to drag you down.

Another way to use your sense of hearing is to immerse yourself in a sound bath. You'll probably need a class for this, either locally or online. They use sounds such as gongs and bowls that actually change brainwave states so you're more relaxed and open (Silverton, 2020). If you've never done one of these before, try it. You may be amazed at how it changes your perspective!

- *Get outside*

Humans are drawn to nature, and being outside is a high-vibe activity. If you exercise outside, now you're providing yourself with a double whammy of high vibration. Even sitting outside away from technology will give you a mood boost and increase your frequency.

- *Put your phone down*

In order to manifest your dream partner, you have to focus with laser-like attention on what it is that you want. All the positive thinking exercises, affirmations, and meditations are about focus. The Law of Attraction won't work for you if you're not dedicated to the project.

If you're constantly checking your phone, you're not able to focus. Period. Especially not on your dream lover.

When you're interrupted at a task, it can take up to 25 minutes to get back into focus (Thorne, 2020). If you're meditating, or looking at your vision board, or visualizing your soulmate and you're interrupted by your phone notifications, you've just wasted almost half an hour. Just by briefly looking at your phone.

Not to mention, being on social media all the time makes you feel lonelier and worse off. In other words, guaranteed to depress you and your vibrational energy, which is the exact opposite of what you're trying to do (Mammoser, 2018). So make sure that you take time away from your laptop, phone, tablet, etc. and spend it doing high-vibrational activities instead.

CHAPTER SUMMARY

We all have a natural frequency at which we resonate, and an important component of manifesting your dream partner is to raise your frequency. There are many techniques for doing so, and they're good for your health in general as well.

- Positive affirmations are short, powerful statements that you repeat to remind yourself that you are deserving of love and that you will manifest your soulmate.
- There are many ways that you can think positively to raise your vibration even if you're not good at it quite yet.
- Manifesting meditation is a special type of meditation that allows you to focus on your ideal partner while you're in an open and relaxed state.
- Raising your vibration is especially powerful when you also involve your senses and your body,

such as practicing yoga, playing music, and exercising outdoors.

IN THE NEXT CHAPTER YOU WILL LEARN HOW TO overcome the obstacles that are blocking you from manifesting your dream partner.

CHAPTER FOUR: OVERCOMING OBSTACLES

As necessary as it is to stay positive and surround yourself with high-vibration people and environments, you still may have barriers that prevent you from manifesting your dream partner. Fortunately many of them are in your mind, which means that with some work on your part, you can eliminate them.

Most obstacles that people face revolve around negativity. They're not sure they can actually achieve their dreams, or they have difficulty removing negativity from the people and objects around them. By the end of this chapter, you'll know which hurdles are in your way and how to overcome them.

OBSTACLES ARE NATURAL

A key thing to remember when you're faced with hindrances is that they're quite common and you should expect them to appear. Some, like limiting beliefs (which we'll discuss in detail shortly) are things that you bring with you into your search for a dream partner.

But others are just interferences that may come up

randomly. Life has ups and downs, so it's not too surprising that the path to your dream partner is not a straight line to happiness!

Accept that interruptions occur. No one grows as a person by staying in their comfort zone. These blockages are actually a way for you to become a better person and a better match for your ideal partner. Only by attempting new things that you've never tried before, and are uncertain about, can you achieve any kind of success in life. That includes your career and personal life, as well as your romantic life.

Sometimes just trying something new can help you overcome the things in your way. Anything small, like driving a new route to work, or maybe biking to work instead of driving. These don't have anything to do with your dream partner, but they do increase your confidence. As you become more confident, the hurdles don't seem quite as high. You'll feel more strongly that you can figure out how to get around or over them.

HURDLES ARE IMPORTANT SIGNS OF PROGRESS

They may seem daunting, but they act as signposts as well. When you're on the verge of manifestation, you'll often see new challenges. If you're a videogame player, you know that the end of one level contains the hardest obstacle in that level. It must be defeated before you can ascend to the next one.

Rather than seeing obstacles as impossible or wallowing in doubts about whether you can get over them, view them as signs that you're getting closer to your dreams. That should help spur you on to defeat them. If manifesting your dream partner was easy, everyone on the planet would be walking around arm-in-arm with their soulmate. It's not easy, and you must push through to achieve your goal.

When you see challenges as opportunities instead, you'll avoid quitting. Because if you do give up, you will not have your dream partner. You've got to keep going, even when the path is rough, and even when the barriers seem too high. You can get over them, with some thinking and planning.

Manifestation doesn't always happen overnight, as we've discussed. It takes some time. Thomas Edison and Albert Einstein had to struggle for years and endure tons of "doesn't quite work" until they were able to uncover their world-changing ideas and theories. Pro athletes train for years before they make it to the big leagues and the Olympics. They put the work in, just as you put the work into your dreams.

They all had blockages in their ways that they had to deal with, and so will you. Some of these obstacles are external, but some of them are internal. They're what you have to sort out in your own mind before your dreams are achievable, such as limiting beliefs.

LIMITING BELIEFS

What are beliefs, to begin with? They're things that you hold to be true, whether or not you have facts or other evidence to back them up. They may be true, or they may not be true.

Limiting beliefs are very common, and not just for those who are using the Law of Attraction (LoA) to manifest their dreams! These types of beliefs constrain us from becoming the people we want to be. They lock people into falsely thinking they can't do something, or that they can't be or have something they want. Usually they are not true, even though people think they are.

Examples of limiting beliefs include

- *Defining who you are by what you do or don't do*

By defining who you are by your position or job, you have a very narrow definition of who you are that doesn't allow for your whole being. For example, if you say, "I do financial analysis," your mind sees you as an analyst. Not as a marketer or artist or whatever else you happen to be.

Or you may think to yourself that you don't date, or you're a person who doesn't date. Then when you have an opportunity, you might skip it. Because you're not a person who dates. And how are you going to find your dream partner without dating?

- *Whether you deserve things*

If you don't believe that you deserve love, you will not be able to manifest your soulmate. You may judge yourself harshly, as most of us are our own worst critics. You made a mistake or did something wrong, so you believe you don't deserve a dream partner or a job or a promotion.

Many people have a transactional idea about who deserves what. So-and-so did a good deed, so they deserve to have something good. Which means if you make a mistake, which you likely perceive as bad, then you don't deserve something good.

But when you're ready to manifest your ideal lover, you'll see that you deserve love. We're all born on this earth deserving love. If you believe in an abundant universe with abundant love, you'll know that you deserve it.

- *Am/ am not*

Similar to the do/don't limiting belief, if you tell yourself that you are an artist, then you close yourself off to having abilities in science or being able to do manual work.

If you define yourself as a single person alone, how will you be able to manifest your dream partner? If your definition is that you exist by yourself, your mind isn't open to the possibility of being part of a couple.

* *Can't/won't*

When you tell yourself that you can't do something, you're absolutely right! When you claim that you can't, you're making sure you never take the steps to do it. For example, if you say "I can't play piano", then you won't take lessons or try to find a piano teacher.

I think you can see where this is going! If you say, "I can't find my soulmate", then you won't be doing your positive affirmations and exercises. Or opening up your space to have a partner living with you.

* *Should/shouldn't*

Honestly, most people would be better off eliminating these words from their vocabulary entirely. These are terrible words that just make you feel bad about not accomplishing things.

These usually mean that you're living by someone else's rules. Because if there was something you wanted to do, you would go ahead and do it. But when you say you "should", it's often because you perceive that someone else thinks it's valuable. Yet it takes the place of something you'd rather be doing.

* *Others are/aren't*

People guess what others are thinking and use those guesses (which are often wrong) to guide their interactions. If you think someone is selfish, or somehow superior to you, you may not want to ask them for help. But they might be thrilled to be asked, because most people love to help.

- *How the world works*

Your beliefs about how the world works can also be very limiting. If you believe that cats hate people and scratch them all the time, you might not want to adopt a perfectly nice feline cuddlebug from the shelter. If you believe that poor people are bad, you're less willing to help them get back on their feet or to learn anything from them.

Understanding how the world works when it comes to love is particularly important for anyone who's searching for their dream partner. You need to know that the universe is abundant in love, and that the more love you give the more you will get. Otherwise, you won't be able to attract your soulmate.

COMMON LIMITING BELIEFS

A bit later in this chapter we'll talk about how you can let go of them, because they will prevent you from attracting your dream partner. Be honest, even if it's only to yourself. Get real about them. That way you'll be able to correct them and start thinking positively about your life and bringing someone new into it. Here are some beliefs that many people hold about love.

1. "I don't deserve love."
2. "I'm not worthy of a partner who loves me the way I want to be loved."

3. "I don't have enough [something] for my dream partner."
4. "I won't be able to handle having a soulmate."
5. "There isn't enough love to go around, and either I don't deserve to have some, or I'll give it up so someone else can have it."
6. "I'm never going to find my soulmate, so why should I try?"

Did any of those resonate with you? How many are "true" for you - meaning that they're something you believe about yourself?

WHY AND HOW WE DEVELOP LIMITING BELIEFS

How do people get things so wrong? It's usually one or more of the following factors. Understanding why you believe what you believe can help you work to overcome these false beliefs.

- *Education*

Many of our beliefs are from what we learned in childhood, from parents, teachers, and peers. If you were always "the pretty one" and your sister was "the smart one", you'll grow up believing that you're not very bright and shouldn't try to do the things that smart people do, like get advanced degrees or work as a professor. Your sister believes that she's not pretty so she may not even try to have a partner, or she might settle for the first one that comes along.

If you didn't do well in school, your parents and teachers might have told you that you wouldn't amount to anything. You've never tried hard to do things, because you believed that you couldn't.

- *Experience*

As people grow older and have their own experiences, they draw conclusions based on what happened that might be faulty. For example, an aspiring writer might submit their short story to a publication and get rejected. They might draw the conclusion that they can't write, and try to do something else.

If you've had bad luck in dating, you might have concluded that you're not a good date, or that it will be hard to find someone to love you. When in fact you may have just had a string of bad luck on dates!

- *Excuses*

It's only in certain forward-thinking technology companies that failure is not only accepted but encouraged. Fail fast so you can take what worked and leave behind what didn't work to try the next thing.

But most people feel bad when they fail at something. They make up excuses to explain away the failure. The problem is that there might have been something to learn in the failure.

Suppose that when you failed at dating, you excused it by saying that you didn't really want to have those dates anyway, you just went on them to make your mother feel better. But what if the real reason that you failed is because you kept choosing people who weren't right for you? By making the excuse you won't try to figure out why you kept choosing the wrong partner. Which would be important to know for someone who's trying to manifest their dream partner!

- *Faulty logic*

It's pretty common for people to fail at logic. Their premises might be wrong, or they might draw conclusions incorrectly. For example, the writer who decided they couldn't write based on one rejection may have drawn the wrong conclusion. Maybe the correct conclusion was that the story wasn't right for that particular publication, and they should submit it to a different one and continue writing.

If you go on a lot of dates but nothing happens, you might draw the false conclusion that you're not pretty enough, or interesting or good enough, to have a romantic partner. But maybe the conclusion should be that you're picking the wrong people for dates. Or that you can't get a second date because on the first one your partner can't get a word in edgewise because you can't stop talking. Or, your partner has to handle the entire conversational load because you didn't say a word the entire night!

- *Fear*

This is a biggie. Plenty of people are afraid to go after what they want. Because they don't deserve it, or someone else deserves it more, or they're afraid of being rejected, or they're afraid their world will turn topsy-turvy if they do get it. There are a lot of different fears that people have that will prevent them from manifesting their desire.

How to overcome limiting beliefs

One thing that many people don't realize is that it's often actually easier for people to stay in limiting beliefs, rather than positive ones.

Because of the way that our brains are wired, we remember bad experiences. They tend to be more vivid and stick in our memories much more than the pleasant ones

(Warner, 2007). When humans were on the savannah, our brains needed to pay much more attention to possible threats to avoid being eaten by tigers. While people don't need to worry about being attacked by tigers anymore, our brains have retained that special attention to threats. Negative experiences remain much stickier than positive ones.

That just means that you may need to work on getting rid of these limiting beliefs and ensure that you pay special attention to the positive. Over time it will become a habit, but at the beginning you might need to put some extra energy and focus into the positive. Here are some methods you can use to overcome the hindrance of limiting beliefs.

- *Mindfulness*

It's important to acknowledge when these types of beliefs rear their ugly heads. If you identified with any of the common beliefs listed above, notice when they come up for you. Or you might notice when you hear the words can't, should, shouldn't, don't come out of your mouth, or appear in your thoughts.

When they pop up, ask yourself if the belief is true. Or is it a thought that came out of the blue? Did it come up as the result of a habit?

If you're your own harshest critic, you've probably developed a habit of telling yourself that you're not enough or that you don't deserve good things. Remember that the universe has love in abundance. That means both that you're enough just as you are, and that you do deserve good things.

Yes, even though you make mistakes and aren't a perfect person. The universe does not require that people be perfect to have good things. Because then no one would ever have anything good. People aren't perfect and the universe respects this.

And if the universe respects the fact that you're not perfect, why don't you?

- *Self-compassion*

Understanding that you're not perfect, and that's OK, is important for self-compassion. When you beat yourself up all the time, over mistakes that you made or things you said or things you didn't say, how can you attract your dream partner?

Recall that like attracts like. Don't beat yourself up over beating yourself up! (Yes, that happens.) Gently bring yourself back to kindness. You may have developed a habit of not being kind to yourself, and it'll take a little time to change the habit. Time and practice will get you to where you need to go, so start practicing kindness. Catch yourself when you're mean to yourself and others and bring kindness back.

- *4-step release*

We got you started with some common limiting beliefs above, but there may be more that you can think of. Now that you know what these types of beliefs are, dig around and see if you can find any others. Repeat the 4-step process for each belief that you find.

1. Write down the limiting belief

Write it down in your own words. Earlier we discussed the importance of writing, and it's still key here. You need to be able to get it down on paper and look at it. Leaving it in your head doesn't work.

2. Recognize that it's a belief, not a truth

The author Evelyn Waugh wrote that we get to keep the limitations we argue for (James, 2013.) Do you want to keep the beliefs that will prevent you from attracting your dream partner? No? Then recognize that the things you've been saying to yourself are not true. Even if you've been repeating them for years.

They may be habits, or thoughts the brain just randomly generated, but that doesn't make them true.

3. Find a different belief

What belief would serve you? Rather than "I'm not deserving of love", you would believe that you do deserve love. Or, "Now that I've spent so much time thinking I don't deserve love, I've recognized that I can have it, because thinking I didn't deserve it didn't get me anywhere."

You need a belief that feels true to you, so if you can't quite get to "I deserve it" yet, try for something positive that moves you in that direction.

4. Act as if the new belief is true

Your old belief was that you were going to fail. Your new belief is that you're going to try for a dream partner, because why not? If you really are the kind of person who tries to attract a soulmate, what kinds of parties do you go to? What do you do when friends invite you to meet people? How do you arrange your space? What do you think about?

- *3-step daily correction*

Know what your limiting beliefs are and accept that you have them, at least for now. An unconscious part of you is holding on to these beliefs that are guiding you toward failure, toward not attracting your soulmate. Each day, be mindful of this belief or set of beliefs if you haven't accepted the new ones yet.

On a daily basis, look within yourself to see how much of the limiting belief still exists.

1. Understand that a part of you is still driving toward failure.
2. Decide to notice when these thoughts occur.
3. When you notice it, accept that it has occurred and then challenge it. Is it true? Replace it with the new belief as in the 4-step process above.

SCARCITY MINDSET

Another obstacle that's mostly in your head is having a scarcity mindset rather than an abundant one. Like the limiting beliefs, you may have been taught these by your parents, or even by your experiences growing up. The problem with scarcity is that you can't think positively, or even see what possibilities are open to you. You'll miss opportunities that have the potential to get you further down the road to your true love.

If this is how you think now, it's understandable, but it's also got to change. The doubts you have about whether you're enough or if you can have enough show up as energy against your dream. The LoA works on the intention with the most energy.

There are a number of methods you can use to switch towards abundance. They won't work immediately because you'll need to practice. As with positive thinking, however, the more you can do them the easier they'll be.

- *Organize - and not just your house*

When you go through your closets and drawers, you might be shocked at how much you actually have. You don't need it all, and you can toss or donate what you don't need. It opens up not just the physical space, but mental and emotional space to bring in your soulmate.

When you look through your daily calendar and note down how much you spend working, you might be surprised how abundant your time actually is too. Instead of frittering it away scrolling on social media (don't feel bad, we all do it), you could open that time up for more productive tasks like visualizing and meditating. Things you might have thought you didn't have time for.

- *Talk with others about things you appreciate*

It's fun to listen to friends and family talk about what they appreciate. Maybe they'll say something that triggers appreciation in you. Being able to talk about the things that you appreciate may make you realize that you do have more than you thought. It's hard to think about what's good in your life when you're feeling negative. Talking to someone else about all the good things brings you into a positive state.

- *Share (your mom was right!)*

This is another concept that's very hard to consider when you're in the throes of a scarcity mindset. It may seem ridiculous to share at this time. You're feeling like you have to grab tight of anything you've got, since that's all you're going to get.

Which is why it's so important to share when you think

it's insane. Not just things, which are good to share, but also time and knowledge and friendship.

You'll get a dopamine boost just from knowing that you've helped someone else out, which will make you feel better. You'll also probably find that you don't miss it and that the sharing was worth it.

And of course you'll find more people sharing with you the more that you share. When that happens, the concept of abundance won't seem so silly.

- *Reduce screen time*

Ads, which are on most screens except maybe e-readers, are all about kindling desire for something that you don't already possess. Practically the exact definition of scarcity. The more time you spend watching TV or scrolling through social media platforms, the more ads you'll be exposed to. You might think you're not paying attention, but every little flash or animation or beep draws you toward it.

You'll also benefit by freeing up time to spend things you like to do and that make you feel happy: crafts, hobbies, hanging out with family and friends. Going to dating groups and otherwise putting yourself in places where you're more likely to meet your mate.

- *Don't compare your insides to someone else's outsides*

This is too easy to do on social media platforms. Everyone curates their feeds, so you see the perfect picture of your friends who are married with their adorable, clean kids and perfectly decorated house. It just makes you feel bad.

What you don't see is that they cleaned up the house for the first time in weeks because the parents were coming over. You didn't see the fifty pictures that were taken with someone's eyes closed, someone running away from the camera, someone (OK, usually one of the kids) with their mouths wide open screaming at the top of their lungs.

You don't see the argument that your friends had the night before, or the fact that someone was sleeping on the sofa. Or that someone didn't sleep because the kids were crying all night. That one shot does not represent the whole of anyone's life, so don't make yourself feel bad by thinking it is. No one has a perfect life, no matter what their social media looks like.

- *Look for the lessons*

As you know, in life, "stuff" happens. No one's life is perfect, and most people's lives are full of ups and downs, good things and bad. When you do come across a loss or a frustration or a failure, try to learn from it. Those things don't make you a bad person or a failure, they make you human. Find the lesson in the experience and use that to improve what you can.

- *Focus on win-wins*

Practically the definition of abundance! Everyone can win.

Life is not pie. If I take my full share, that doesn't mean you or anyone else has less. This is the secret to negotiation: coming up with a solution that is a win for both parties. Even if neither can get everything they want.

As much as you can, create situations where everyone can shine. Potluck dinners (and everyone helps the host clean up)? Allot tasks so that everyone gets something they're at least reasonably good at? Thank everyone who helped you, when you're thanked for something? The more wins you can spread around for everyone, the better. And the more wins others will seek to give you too.

- *Gratitude journal*

Similar to talking about the things you appreciate, writing down what you're grateful for will remind you that you do have many things in your life. Even if you don't yet have your dream partner. You have love in the form of family, friends, and possibly pets. You're probably thankful for the roof over your head and clothes on your back, even if they're not fancy or expensive.

What happened during the day that you can be thankful for? Once you start thinking about them, you may be surprised by how many little moments brought you some happiness during the day. Write them down to help you remember all the little things. And so that when you're feeling down, you can look through the pages and remember that you have so many positive things in your life.

FOCUSING ON THE DON'TS INSTEAD OF THE DOS

Although you know by now how important it is to laser in on the positive aspects instead of the negative, sometimes you'll find it's hard to avoid the don'ts.

The easiest way to clear this hurdle is to make sure that you have the right morning routine. Hint: your phone is nowhere near where you sleep. Even if you use your phone for guided meditation, it needs to be located in a separate room when you're sleeping.

Remember that when you sleep, your vibrational frequency is neutral. If you start your day off with negativity, you'll drop it for the entire day. Why do that if you don't have to? Instead, when you wake up, raise your vibration by setting your intention to think positive right away. Do nothing else before you set this positive intention.

Follow up immediately with a gratitude practice. Write your thoughts down in a journal. If you can't quite get to the point where you're writing the first thing in the morning, at least think of three things that you're grateful for. These should come pretty quickly. Don't spend too much time thinking about whether you're more grateful for this or for that. Just three quick things that you're thankful for having in your life, and then off you go.

RESISTANCE

Our brains are interesting things! There's a lot that goes on in the human subconscious, and the conscious mind has no idea what's happening. However, the brain does send signals that people can learn to notice to tell them that something deeper is going on. Fears and doubts that haven't quite made it into the conscious area of the brain show up as resistance.

On the surface, you're opening up your heart, you've done the T-chart, you've made physical and emotional space and yet, nothing's happening. You've got two intentions going, and you're unaware of the subconscious one. The intention you think you're working on is manifesting your dream partner, and the other one is directed toward your fears.

The Law of Attraction works on the intention that you have more energy toward, which is usually the subconscious. It operates faster, more often and more energetically than the conscious. Ignoring what's happening doesn't work, because your subconscious can't ignore it. Instead, deal with the resistance so you can let the fears and doubts go.

You're probably wondering how to overcome the resistance if it's all there in your subconscious! Imagine that you've manifested your dream partner, and you're living that life. How does it affect your other relationships, such as with your friends and family? What impact does it have on your career? Will it change your health, location, purpose? Think of all the different ways in which your life will change. All the side effects that will come from having this new person in your life.

Notice the side effects without judging them. You might want to write them down in your journal to make sure that you can grab hold of them. These are the secret fears and anxieties that are currently hiding out in your subconscious. You might be worried that your family won't like the new partner. Maybe because you've chosen someone different from who they want for you. Or you have a friend who will no longer be such a big part of your life, now that you have a partner. You worry about single friends that you think will be angry with you for leaving the friend group. Or you're thinking of living somewhere else with your dream partner, and you're concerned about losing your job that you enjoy.

There are a lot of ways in which your life may change once you have a dream partner, and it's important to acknowledge them so that they can then be resolved. Do remember that the consequences you're envisioning are potential ones. Just like limiting beliefs, they're not necessarily true.

Overcoming resistance

Now that you know you have some unconscious concerns that are getting in the way of manifesting your dream partner, you can take action to resolve them.

- *Use it to your advantage*

When possible, try to turn the resistance to your advantage. Look for ways to soothe the concerns you have without succumbing to them.

If you're concerned about moving somewhere else, research the new place online and go visit it. You'll see whether it's a place you truly want to live, and you'll be able to decide whether or not you really want to move there.

- *Reframe negative thoughts*

The first step is to notice when you're thinking negative things, which may take some practice. You want to transform them into positive thoughts.

But that doesn't mean that you ignore the negative ones and think of random positive ones instead. Once you've noticed them, acknowledge them. Thoughts and emotions in your brain don't go away just because you ignore them. In fact, that usually makes things worse!

Don't exaggerate the negative, but state it clearly. Notice how it feels to make the acknowledgement, and now you can shift to a more positive belief.

For example, if you're worried that your friend will be upset if you start spending more time with your dream partner, notice that thought when it arrives. "I know [my friend] will be upset with me when I can't spend as much time with them, and that makes me nervous. It's a sign that they care about me and want to hang out with me. At the same time, this is my life. I can still spend some time with them if I like, and I'm not responsible for how other people feel. The person I need to please is me, and I am looking forward to my life with my dream partner."

- *Keep an eye on your mood*

Try to notice when the negative thoughts or feelings arise. It's easier to let your worries go when you know they're occurring. An easy signal that resistance is happening is your bad mood! Let that be your guide to noticing what's bubbling up from your subconscious.

- *Raise your vibration*

Negativity decreases your vibration. Once you raise it, you'll be in a better mood. Focus on positive ideas and have some fun as we discussed in chapter three. Lift yourself out of the stressed, unhappy mood that resistance puts you in.

NEGATIVE THINKING OR FEELING STATES

Sometimes people, despite their best intentions, lose the positivity they need to keep practicing to manifest their dreams. They fall into feelings of negativity, or end up in a low or even no vibration frequency. It's important to shake these off as soon as you can.

It's common to start the day off feeling strong and with good intentions. But as the day goes on and things happen, the vibration might start dropping. It's important to keep a tally of everything that went right during the day, every day. Like attracts like and wins attract wins, so the more you can jot down, the more you'll have in the future. That will help you keep your motivation up. You might also need to counteract the natural afternoon slump that happens to many people with a short burst of exercise or a short meditation to help you recharge.

It's also helpful to reach out and ask for help when you're having difficulty with low vibration states. It's not a sign of weakness, but of strength that you're able to see you need some objective help.

The other thing you can do is take action to raise your vibration very quickly. It doesn't require any prep. Keep this list handy for times when you just want to get out of your negativity fast. They are suggestions that you can do on the spur of the moment and they'll help you feel more positive immediately.

- Throw on some tunes and dance
- Take a bath with Epsom salts
- Verbally say one thing that you're grateful for, that instant. Yes, you have to say it out loud.
- Meditate
- Take deep breaths
- Create some art, whatever art is for you
- Hug it out
- Go out in nature and feel the water of the lake or ocean, or the grass or soil under your feet
- Notice something beautiful to you
- Clean up

CAN THE LAW OF ATTRACTION FAIL?

You may be wondering, after reading up this point, if it's possible for the LoA to fail. Or just not work for you specifically. It definitely will not work if your vibration isn't high enough to match your intent. In other words, if you have resistance you haven't dealt with, or you don't believe it will work, or that the universe is abundant enough to help you attract your soulmate. It doesn't work when your energy is shifted toward another intention, whether or not you realize that's the case.

There are some other reasons why you haven't yet manifested your ideal partner.

- *Believe that positive thinking is enough*

As they say, thinking affirmatively is a condition that's necessary but not sufficient. If you don't think positively, you won't get the ideal partner that you've been waiting for. But you have to do more than just think constructively.

You can't ignore the negative thoughts and try to banish them, or squash them down someplace deep where you hope they'll never come up. Because they will.

- *Where is my dream mate already??*

Impatience is a sign that you don't really believe the Law of Attraction works. If you understand abundance, you know that it's coming. Visualizing, vision boards, and positive affirmations aren't enough for attracting your dream partner if you doubt that the LoA will work.

- *Dwell on what's gone wrong*

Constantly staying in negativity doesn't help either. The more you harp on things that didn't go the way you want them, the farther away from your dream partner you'll be. Your energy is focused on what went wrong, which drops your vibration. You'll only attract more negativity thinking and talking in this manner.

Now is the time to ask yourself what benefit you're getting from this kind of talk. If you weren't getting any benefit, you'd stop, so what is the purpose? Are you hanging out with negative people who enjoy hearing the negativity? Does it help you feel like you're in control? Or maybe you're getting validation from those who listen and commiserate with you?

Be honest about what you're receiving. Then you can

decide how to achieve those benefits from positivity instead. At that point you can act to raise your vibration back where it needs to be.

- *Don't recognize the signals that you're on the verge of manifestation*

When you haven't yet manifested what you've been visualizing and working toward, it's pretty common to misread the signals. For example, if you're manifesting a new place to live, a realtor's sign going up next door to you is a signal.

In terms of your soulmate, seeing happy couples hand-in-hand is a sign that manifestation is near for you. It may not feel like it! But this is a positive sign, and you need to express your appreciation for it.

Note that all of these are not failures of LoA. They're not exactly failures of yours, either. They just mean that you have some additional work to do, around positive thinking or abundance mindset or recognizing and resolving your resistance. You could very well have more than one subconscious fear or concern about attracting your dream partner, and you'll need to resolve all of them before you can attract your soulmate.

Negative signs mean that your vibration is not matched to your intention. You'll need to do some detective work to figure out what you need to fix to get back into the right groove.

Chapter Summary

There are a number of reasons why your dream partner hasn't come into your life (yet), and most of them stem from your thinking or your subconscious anxieties and worries.

There are concrete steps you can take to address these issues, so that you can bring your vibration up.

- Obstacles may be higher than they appear, but they're often signs that manifestation is near and you can conquer them if you take the right attitude.
- One type of barrier is a limiting belief, which constrains you from the positive belief that you need in this situation.
- Many people experience resistance, which is the result of subconscious fears that need to be resolved before the LoA can work.
- Negative states and feelings also need to be overcome.
- When you're not manifesting your dream partner, it's usually because there is some hidden issue that you need to discover and resolve in order to let the universe know that you're ready.

IN THE NEXT CHAPTER WE'LL PUT EVERYTHING together for a complete system to attract your dream partner.

CHAPTER FIVE: PUTTING ALL THE PIECES OF THE PUZZLE TOGETHER: 8 STEPS TO MANIFEST YOUR DREAM PARTNER

So far in the book we've provided you with the fundamental information that you need to understand how the Law of Attraction (LoA) works and how to manifest your soulmate. Now we're going to put it all together and create an action plan for you to let the power of the universe work to your advantage. You have all the pieces you need for the puzzle.

As we've discussed, reading about it isn't enough. Thinking positively isn't enough. There are actions that you'll need to take in order to attract your dream partner. Your energy and the focus of your attention must be on this manifestation, or else it will not work. Recall that like attracts like. If your energy is focused on anything else, that's what the universe will send. Only by maintaining a high vibrational energy will you achieve what you desire.

And when your vibration is high and you're finding the positive in life, you'll be rewarded. The good energy that you bring to your manifestation is actually good for you in general. Working on attracting your dream partner might be even better for you than you originally hoped.

You might have noticed in the discussion about obstacles that some of the remedies are common to many of the hurdles that you might meet, and are also in the chapter on raising your vibration. That's a signal that these things should be in your daily routine, and possibly more than once during your day.

- *Exercise*

Especially outdoors, it's a key way to lift your mood as well as raise your vibration anytime. When the afternoon slump hits, many people eat something sweet or drink a coffee milkshake to get some energy. Both those things do provide a quick hit of energy, which is usually followed by a serious energy crash. They both also cause inflammation in your body.

Instead, try going for a quick walk. It doesn't have to be long or arduous. If it's too hot or wet or cold outside, see if you can take a walk around the building or do some stairs.

Exercise also works when you're starting to feel stressed out or overwhelmed. Sometimes stomping up and down a flight of stairs is exactly what you need to get back to your good vibration!

- *Meditation*

Calming and opening your mind helps you to destress. It also makes space for what you're trying to manifest. Top performers of all kinds, from athletes to business people, use meditation in their daily practice.

- *Gratitude practice*

Unfortunately it's so easy for us to get caught up in the

negative and unconstructive, given the way that our brains are wired. A written gratitude practice is a good way to combat this. You can do it either in the morning or at night, but each day it's important to note what you're thankful for.

If you do it in the morning, it sets you up to notice things during the day that you're grateful for. At night, it reminds you of all the good things that happened during the day. Either way, when you're feeling down or having difficulty with thankfulness, you can come back to your written journal and remind yourself of all the things you have going for you.

- *Reframing to be constructive*

Despite the fact that you do need positive thoughts in your mind to attract your soulmate, sometimes your mind is going to think negative thoughts. Acknowledging them so they don't build up in your subconscious to create resistance is important. Also be able to reframe them into something affirmative that makes sense to you.

It's important, and not just for Law of Attraction practices. It helps you realize your full potential in anything you do, so that your thoughts can't hold you back.

STEPS TO MANIFESTING YOUR DREAM PARTNER

Putting it all together, the process is pretty simple. Just remember that simple doesn't always mean easy! You will have to put some effort into this if you're expecting to attract your soulmate.

1. Identify your ideal partner

Who is your dream partner? What do you want from

your soulmate? You're not looking for your list of "don't wants", although creating that list will help you figure out what it is that you do want.

Once you know what you want, the universe can provide it. Most people want a "nice" person for their soulmate, but what does that mean to you? In your eyes, what does a nice person do, and how do they act?

Get specific about your ideal mate. Not in terms of height or weight, but in terms of characteristics: funny, honest, reliable, etc. Be very clear about what you want. After all, you'll be attracting this person to you for the rest of your life. Make sure that it's really what you want. Not necessarily what your parents or friends or family want for you.

2. Visualize in rich detail

Picture your life with your soulmate, in as much detail as you possibly can. Not just what it looks like, but also what it smells and tastes and sounds like.

And crucially, what does it feel like? What are the emotions that occur when you have your dream partner by your side? Are you content, excited, joyful, serene? Bring those into your picture as well.

Develop a vision board that captures all this detail. You'll want to add to it on a regular basis, and make changes whenever they're necessary to it as well. Keep it in a spot where your eyes are naturally drawn to it. Don't hide it in a cupboard or closet.

You may also want to purchase (or make) things that represent the life you'll lead together. If you want to travel, pick up brochures for interesting destinations. If you'll be moving to the beach, try scattering some seashells around your home and buy a beach umbrella for your (current) patio.

3. Create a daily routine to raise your vibration

Use all the affirmative ways to raise your vibration that make sense for you, and create a daily routine.

In the chapter on raising your vibration, we listed a lot of ways to make sure that you keep a high vibration and a positive outlook. The universe will provide what your energy is drawn to, and your vibration must be high enough to match that of your ideal mate.

Many of these methods work better with repetition. Creating a daily routine around them will help you make sure you're getting in your reps. Just as you get your reps in at the gym! Have a few things that you do in the morning before you look at screens or check email, such as deep breathing, meditation, and positive affirmations. For a short time each day, multiple times a day, practice your visualization and look at your vision board.

If you have a very structured day, you may want to pinpoint exact times when you'll do something like study your vision board and meditate. Otherwise, you can set alarms or notifications on your phone to remind you so you don't forget.

4. Identify any obstacles currently in your path

It's common to have limiting beliefs, or hidden fears and worries, that prevent the attraction of a soulmate. Sometimes it's the specific imagining that brings up the fears and anxieties that cause resistance.

It's also normal to have beliefs that constrain you from focusing your attention on your dream mate the way you need to. You may not believe that you're deserving of love, or that there's enough love in the world to go around. Or that you'll never be able to find your soulmate.

5. Remove or go around the obstacles

Work on these issues. Most people are their own worst enemies, so you'll probably find that your biggest problem stems from you. The good news is that you can solve these problems once you know you have them.

Another important lesson is that very often, barriers that suddenly appear are signs that you're closer to your dreams. The universe will often throw in a test to make sure that you're really ready to accept your soulmate into your life. Attacking them is a way to raise your vibration and show that you are ready for your manifestation.

6. Continue to keep vibrations high

As things come up, use what you've learned and refer back to this book to find ideas on getting yourself out of low vibration situations. Acknowledge where you are, and then fix it. If you notice you're in a sudden slump, you can try one of the quick ways to make yourself feel better, such as an impromptu single dance party.

Address these unproductive thoughts, feelings, and circumstances as they arise. Don't let them fester, or even worse, attach too much meaning to them. Sometimes the brain makes some silly thoughts, so let them go and don't dwell on them.

When you find you are dwelling on something, ask yourself what the benefit is for doing so. Then find a positive way to get that same benefit and that will help you get closer to your goal.

7. Find ways to be in an attractive situation

How can you make it easy and obvious for the universe

to bring your ideal mate to you? Earlier in the book, you learned about decluttering and making space for another person in your house. Repainting, rearranging furniture, etc.

But there are other ways to be attractive to your dream partner. You will not get your soulmate by sitting inside your house all day! You must get out into places where your dream partner might be.

If you have a hobby that you'll share, go to meetings and events and conferences around the hobby. Join groups online, and go to in-person events as well. Attend parties where there will be other single people, and maybe networking events if you want to attract a businessperson.

Being attractive also refers to improving yourself where appropriate. Best if it also involves socializing! For example, suppose you want to be able to speak confidently in public. Join a Toastmasters group near you. If you want to learn another language, especially if your ideal mate also speaks it, join a conversation club.

Or, if you plan to be with someone who loves the water, you might take group lessons for paddleboarding, sailing, kayaking, waterskiing, etc. When you're the active type, make sure you're in a rec league or Masters league for your chosen sport.

8. Manifest!

Watch for the signs that manifestation is coming shortly. Maybe you see your friends getting married, or other single friends finding people to settle down with. Be open to the ways your soulmate appears in your life. You may not recognize them right away, so don't be dismissive of the people that come into your life at this stage.

ACTIONS TO TAKE

A lot of what we've discussed in the book is mental. Much of the effort that you'll be expending is with your mind. Having said that, there are some actions that you need to perform to ensure that you're on the same track as the universe. And that you're sending out the right energy to make sure you get what you want. These are concrete things you can do that will raise your vibration, create the space for another person to join you, and bring you to the places where the universe might place your dream mate.

- *Develop and maintain the vision board*

I won't go into much detail on this, because you've probably got it down already! Don't forget to include the emotions on your board. This can be done as simply as writing out the words and attaching them to the board. Or you can find images that represent these feelings for you.

- *Perform the daily routines*

It's great to think about and create the routines that will help you keep your vibration high, but it's another thing to do them! Many people are in the (bad!) habit of keeping their phone with them in the bedroom and then rolling over and checking it first thing in the morning.

Keeping it out of the bedroom is a good idea in general. Especially when you have a soothing routine set up to help you attract your soulmate. Screens keep people awake because the blue light interferes with the body's circadian rhythm. So charge it somewhere else.

Make sure that whatever you need for your morning (and evening) routine is within easy reach. A glass of water, journal and pen, meditation timer, whatever it is. Make the routine easy so you can quickly create the habit.

- *Create and perform rituals*

Rituals are very important to human beings, as there's evidence of them from way back in human history. They help us maintain a sense of control over what's going on (Hershfield, 2013). Make your visualizations, affirmations and meditations special by creating rituals around them. Soothing music, comfortable seating, and maybe scented candles make the moment feel special.

You can create rituals around meals and other daily routines as well. Try setting the table for dinner in a romantic way, just as you would when your dream partner is present. It's another way of raising your vibration and makes the meal seem special just for you, too.

- *Continue to resolve mental blocks*

Unfortunately, they don't usually go away the first time you deal with them! They tend to return, and you'll need to continue your routine of acknowledging and reframing. Over time they'll occur less frequently.

But if you're new to working with them, expect that they'll rear their ugly heads more often than you'd like.

- *Clean out your house*

Now is the time, if you have a lot of clutter, to get rid of it. Donate or sell what you can, but if it's stained or broken, dump it. If you have a lot of electronic items you'll probably need to take them to a special recycling center, because they can't be thrown out in the trash. Remember that the universe does not take kindly to people destroying the earth!

Having a lot of stuff makes it hard to focus your attention. You're always distracted by something that catches your eye. Or the feeling that you have to clean up.

Plus, by clearing out your things, you're making room for another person's things. Think about what your dream partner might like to have in their pad. If you're a woman looking for a man and you have some very frilly items that your soulmate would probably rather not look at, consider getting rid of them.

Conversely, if you're a man looking for a woman, you might think about getting rid of your excessively masculine items that aren't necessary: beer can collections, taxidermied heads, foam fingers, etc. You get the idea!

- *Arrange the space*

Would your dream partner be comfortable in your place as it is now? People tend to get used to things in their house, so try looking at it as if you were the soulmate. Do you need a bigger sofa to sit on? A bigger bed? Or your furniture might be fine just as it is, but you could make the room bigger by rearranging it.

Maybe you have items that are in the way of easy pathways. Assuming it's something you need and not just clutter, try to find a home for it out of the way. Go through your whole house and make sure that the space is ready for another person to come into it.

- *Act as if*

You've put in a lot of effort into your visualization, and you probably have a very good idea of what life with your soulmate will be like. Act as if you already have your soulmate in your life.

What would a person with an ideal partner do? Go and do likewise. Maybe you would go outside more often, or enjoy making meals at home.

More importantly, act as if the feelings have manifested already. If you know that you will feel more serene with your dream mate in your life, act like a serene person. Such an individual doesn't get upset with the minor accidents and mishaps in everyday life.

They enjoy their food and eat it slowly. They might make a ritual out of eating, with tablecloths and candles and cloth napkins, for example. They get out to commune with nature, and they don't compete with or compare themselves to other people.

- *Purchase (or make) manifestation items*

Please note that this isn't an invitation to spend wildly or go into debt! But you may see items that are made for happy couples, like a frame with wedding rings or wedding bells, that you can pick up for yourself. Buy romantic music too.

Or the lingerie/underwear that you'd love for your dream partner to see you in. Wear it for yourself, as well, because that helps you act as if you have your mate already.

When buying appliances, make sure they're big enough for two people. Don't buy a one-person microwave, buy one that's made for two.

Whatever your hobby or skill is, see where you can fit that into the idea of you plus your soulmate. If you make birdhouses, you can make one that's big enough for two birds, or possibly two houses side-by-side.

Get creative! What speaks to you about happy couples, or

people partnered with their soulmates? See how you can represent that in your house right now.

- *Get out of the house*

After all, you and your dream partner won't spend your entire lives inside the house either! Getting out into nature will help you raise your vibration and feel better.

You also get to meet people face-to-face when you're outside your house. You never know where you're going to find the mate of your dreams! You just might meet a person who brings the two of you together, if not your ideal partner themselves.

- *Join likely groups*

Getting out of the house is a great start to meeting people, but joining groups where your dream partner is likely to hang out or attend is even better. It also helps you develop your social skills, which can only help you attract the right person.

Places where your partner is likely to be include the hobbies and activities that you share. If you're manifesting an avid hiker, you'd join the Sierra Club (or similar) group near to you. You'd also go online to find Meetup or similar groups where hikers gather, and join their events. Remember, you do have to go in person. If there are conferences or other events that target your audience, make sure you attend them.

Larger groups are probably more target-rich environments than smaller ones. If you live in a small town or remote region, you're likely to find more on offer if you travel to the nearest metropolis and join in the groups there. Even if you're specifically looking for someone who prefers small towns and wilderness, you'll have more opportunities in the nearest big town. And there are probably plenty of people there who yearn to live in the wilderness or cozy community that you can offer!

Other groups to join are singles and dating ones. Everyone there is also searching for a partner, so you'll easily find single people. Speed dating, activity groups for singles, date night cruises and events are all places you should try.

In addition to finding your dream partner, you'll also have fun and maybe brush up on skills while you're out there. Now that's a win-win situation!

CHAPTER SUMMARY

The 8-step process for manifestation helps you put together everything you've learned in this book. In addition to all the mental work you're doing, there are actions for you to perform that will help you raise your vibration. And ultimately help you manifest the partner of your dreams.

- Positivity is necessary for the Law of Attraction, and before you can attract your soulmate you'll need to resolve any negativity that gets in your way.
- The 8-step system is simple, which doesn't mean it's necessarily easy, as there may be work you need to do on yourself to make sure you're bringing the right person into your life.
- In addition to the mental work, make sure that you are performing the actions that get you closer to your ideal mate, including acting as-if and making mental and physical space for them.

FINAL WORDS

Hopefully you enjoyed this discussion of the Law of Attraction (LoA) and how it works to bring you the partner you've always dreamed of. You also know that just reading about it isn't enough. The next step is to start using the techniques and the 8-step process of manifesting your soulmate if you haven't already begun. Once you have your ideal partner, you can use the principles in the book to attract any other goal you want to achieve in your life.

We discussed what the LoA means and how it works. You learned that everything has a vibrational energy. In order to manifest a dream partner, you must be a vibrational match. The universe responds to the energy that you put into it, so if your focus is on something else other than your potential lover, that is what you'll attract. Because like attracts like, you can manifest the love of your life only when you're positive. If you're sending out negative energy, the universe will respond to that instead.

You discovered how to find out what you want in your dream partner if you didn't already know. With a T-chart of "wants" and "don't wants", you crossed off all the traits you dislike in a partner to focus on just the constructive ones. Once you found out what your ideal mate is like, you pictured your life with your soulmate in rich detail. Not only what this new life looks like, but what it tastes, smells and sounds like. Most importantly, how it feels. You now understand the importance of emotion in visualization, because that heightens the vibrations you send out. You also created a vision board to study daily.

In the next chapter, we talked about how to raise your vibration. Everyone has a natural vibe at which they resonate. Negativity, destructive thoughts, and other unfavorable issues that crop up drop your vibration below where it needs to be to manifest your desires. The interesting thing is that everything you do to raise your vibration is also good for life in general, such as exercise, meditation, and eating good food. There are positive thinking exercises and affirmations that you add to your daily routine to stay in the right mindset. It's important to match the high vibration of your potential mate since the universe matches up like with like.

After the high vibrations, we uncovered the opposite end of the spectrum: overcoming obstacles. They can be internal or external. Most people are hardest on themselves. Learning to reframe the negative thoughts is an important skill to be able to manifest your dream partner.

Not only are there barriers at the beginning such as your own limiting beliefs, but they can also come up as you're working on the process. Many people don't realize that their subconscious is worrying about the side effects of the new life, and that arises consciously as resistance. You read about some methods you can use to overcome resistance when you've identified it, as well as how to tell when they arrive so you can address them. You also learned that the universe has a habit of tossing up some hurdles when you're close to manifestation, to make sure that you're really ready for what it's about to bring you.

In the last chapter we put all these concepts together in the 8-step process for manifesting your dream partner. Much of it is mental: identifying the characteristics of your soulmate, visualizing your life with them, overcoming the internal obstacles, working through affirmations and positive thinking exercises, etc. But there are other actions to take too. In addition to creating your vision board, you need to act as if you have this life as you've pictured it and arrange your space (mentally and physically) to welcome your ideal mate.

Follow the Law of Attraction process, work the steps, and enjoy your new life when you've manifested the partner of your dreams!

REFERENCES

A. (2019, November 14). 7 Essential Positive Thinking Exercises to Transform Your Life. Retrieved from https://www.applythelawofattraction.com/positive-thinking-exercises/

Abraham, J. (2019, December 4). How to Overcome Obstacles Before Manifestation. Retrieved from https://www.yourpositivereality.com/how-to-overcome-obstacles-before-manifestation/

Ackerman, C. (2020, April 28). What is Neuroplasticity? Retrieved from https://positivepsychology.com/neuroplasticity/

Brown, J. (2019, December 10). The Law of Attraction Uncovered: What is Vibrational Frequency? Retrieved from https://manifesteveryday.com/law-of-attraction-uncovered-what-is-vibrational-frequency/

Campbell, R. (2015, April 17). 17 ways to raise your vibration fast. Retrieved from https://rebeccacampbell.me/ways-to-raise-your-vibration-fast/

Canfield, J. (2019a, October 1). Law of Attraction Guide for Joy, Relationships, Money & More. Retrieved from https://www.jackcanfield.com/blog/using-the-law-of-attraction/

Canfield, J. (2019b, November 26). How To Find Your Soulmate Using the Law of Attraction. Retrieved from https://www.jackcanfield.com/blog/find-soulmate-using-law-attraction/

Changing Minds. (n.d.). Limiting Beliefs. Retrieved May 14, 2020, from http://changingminds.org/explanations/belief/limiting_beliefs.htm

Cooper, C. (2013, March 4). Remove Obstacles. Retrieved from https://carlycoopercoaching.com/remove-obstacles/

Daniels, E. (2019, November 14). You Attract By Vibration. Retrieved from https://www.applythelawofattraction.com/you-attract-vibration/

Daniels, E. (2019, November 14). 5 Great Ways to Overcome Resistance When Using the Law of Attraction. Retrieved from https://www.applythelawofattraction.com/overcome-resistance/

Daniels, E. (2019, November 14). 5 Reasons Why the Law of Attraction Fails to Work. Retrieved from https://www.applythelawofattraction.com/law-attraction-fails/

Dhiraj. (2016, August 28). Law of Attraction Articles blog. Retrieved from https://www.dhirajrajmotivation.com/law-of-attraction-articles

Fox, T. (2019, October 28). 20 LAw of Attraction Exercises to Practise Daily. Retrieved from https://thriveglobal.com/stories/20-law-of-attraction-exercises-to-practise-daily/

Gunter, P. (2020, February 18). Vision Board – A Powerful

Tool To Manifest Your Dream Life. Retrieved from
https://www.thelawofattraction.com/vision-board/

Hamm, T. (2020, April 8). From the Scarcity Mindset to the
Abundance Mindset. Retrieved from
https://www.thesimpledollar.com/financial-wellness/from-
the-scarcity-mindset-to-the-abundance-mindset/

Hershfield, H. (2013, August 29). Why Do We Engage in
Rituals? Retrieved from
https://www.psychologytoday.com/us/blog/the-edge-
choice/201308/why-do-we-engage-in-rituals

Holly. (2020, May 4). The Power Of Writing Affirmations.
Retrieved from https://www.thinktranquility.com/the-power-
of-writing-affirmations/

Hurst, K. (2019, June 5). Law Of Attraction History: The
Origins Of The Law Of Attraction Uncovered. Retrieved
from https://www.thelawofattraction.com/history-law-
attraction-uncovered/

Hurst, K. (2017, December 19). How To Be Optimistic: 15
Positive Thinking Exercises. Retrieved from
https://www.thelawofattraction.com/positive-thinking-
exercises/

Hurst, K. (2016, November 23). Manifestation Guide: How
To Manifest Anything You Want In 24hrs. Retrieved from
https://www.thelawofattraction.com/manifest-something-
want-24hrs-less/

Hurst, K. (2015, November 27). 6 Physical Steps To
Attracting Love: Things You Can Do Right NOW. Retrieved
from https://www.thelawofattraction.com/6-physical-steps-
to-attract-love-right-now/

J. (2020, January 13). What Are Your Biggest Limiting Beliefs?
Retrieved from https://www.habitsforwellbeing.com/what-are-
your-biggest-limiting-beliefs/

James, M. (2013, November 5). 4 Steps to Release "Limiting

Beliefs" Learned From Childhood. Retrieved from https://www.psychologytoday.com/us/blog/focus-forgiveness/201311/4-steps-release-limiting-beliefs-learned-childhood

James, S. (2018, April 29). ABUNDANCE MINDSET vs. SCARCITY MINDSET. Retrieved from https://projectlifemastery.com/abundance-mindset-vs-scarcity-mindset/

Kaplan, D. (2017, May 4). Meditation for Manifesting Your Dreams - And Accomplishing Your Goals. Retrieved from https://www.forbes.com/sites/dinakaplan/2017/04/30/meditation-for-manifesting-your-dreams-and-accomplishing-your-goals/#1c96b8cd36c2

Kathy. (2019, September 12). How To Overcome Obstacles In Your Life. Retrieved from https://magneticlawofattraction.com/how-to-overcome-obstacles-in-your-life/

Law of Attraction. (n.d.). Using Meditation for Manifestation – The Law Of Attraction Library. Retrieved May 11, 2020, from https://thelawofattraction.org/using-meditation-for-manifestation/

Ledwell, N. (n.d.). Discover How To Use The Law of Attraction To Overcome Obstacles in Life. Retrieved May 15, 2020, from https://www.mindmovies.com/blogroll/discover-how-to-use-the-law-of-attraction-to-overcome-obstacles-in-life

Mammoser, G. (2018, December 14). The FOMO Is Real: How Social Media Increases Depression and Loneliness. Retrieved from https://www.healthline.com/health-news/social-media-use-increases-depression-and-loneliness

McGinley, K. (2019, October 23). A Complete Guide to Raise Your Vibration. Retrieved from https://chopra.com/articles/a-complete-guide-to-raise-your-vibration

Palmer, A. (n.d.). The Neuroscience of Visualization. Retrieved May 10, 2020, from https://www.mindmovies.com/blogroll/the-neuroscience-of-visualization

Parienti, S. (2020, March 21). the 5 fastest ways to raise your vibration. Retrieved from https://www.yogitimes.com/article/the-5-fastest-ways-to-raise-your-vibration/

Positivity, P. O. (2019, May 1). 8 Ways to Find Your Soul Mate Using The Law of Attraction. Retrieved from https://www.powerofpositivity.com/find-soul-mate-law-of-attraction/

raise-your-vibration. (n.d.). Yoga Techniques for Raising your Vibration. Retrieved May 12, 2020, from http://www.raise-your-vibration.com/yoga-techniques.html

Ruth, A. (2017, May 4). 8 Ways To Train Your Brain To Become More Positive. Retrieved from https://due.com/blog/train-your-brain-to-become-more-positive/

Seagraves, K. (2019, January 26). Don't Check Your Phone The First Thing In The Morning. Retrieved from https://www.uncoveryourpurpose.com/check-phone-first-thing-morning/

Silverton, L. (2020, February 11). 10 Practical Ways To Raise Your Positive Vibrations. Retrieved from https://www.mindbodygreen.com/0-7823/10-practical-ways-to-raise-your-positive-vibrations.html

Thorne, B. (2020, February 13). How Distractions At Work Take Up More Time Than You Think. Retrieved from http://blog.idonethis.com/distractions-at-work/

Titus. (2019, October 15). 42 Love Affirmations To Attract Love That WORK! Retrieved from https://freshaffirmations.com/love/

VOA Learning English. (2012, November 1). Can You

"Think and Grow Rich?" A Famous Books Says, "Yes." Retrieved from https://learningenglish.voanews.com/a/can-you-think-and-grow-rich-a-famous-book-says-yes/1536923.html

Warner, J. (2007, August 29). Bad Memories Easier to Remember. Retrieved from https://www.webmd.com/brain/news/20070829/bad-memories-easier-to-remember